A Party
of One

Meditations for
Those Who Live Alone

Joni Woelfel

With quotes from *Loving Yourself for God's Sake,*
Sabbath Moments and *Heart Peace*
by Adolfo Quezada

Resurrection Press
An Imprint of
CATHOLIC BOOK PUBLISHING CORP.
Totowa • New Jersey

First published in September 2005 by Resurrection Press, Catholic Book Publishing Corp.

Copyright © 2005 by Joni Woelfel

ISBN 1-933066-01-6

Library of Congress Catalog Card Number: 2005927387

Scripture quotations are from the New Revised Standard Version of the Bible, copyright 1989 by the Division of Christian Education of the National Council of the Churches of Christ in the USA. Used by permission. All rights reserved.

Cover design by Beth DeNapoli

Cover art by Mary Southard, CSJ, © Sisters of St. Joseph of LaGrange

Printed in the United States of America

1 2 3 4 5 6 7 8 9

www.catholicbookpublishing.com

Acknowledgments

I am grateful to the editors of the following publications, in which versions of chapters of this book were originally published, including:

"The Legacy of a Bridge Builder," *Catholic Women's Network,* Fall 2003.

"How to Take Leave," *Catholic Women's Network,* December 2004.

"The Sign of the Shadow," *National Catholic Reporter,* Starting Point, Christmas 2005.

"Opening the Door," *National Catholic Reporter,* Starting Point, March 4, 2004, Vol. 41, #18.

"One Year Rite of Passage," *National Catholic Reporter,* Starting Point, November 26, 2004, Vol. 41, #6.

"The Ides of March," previously published in *The Edge of Greatness, Empowering Meditations for Life,* Joni Woelfel, Resurrection Press, Totowa, NJ, 2004.

Dedication

This book is lovingly dedicated to my sisters
Julie Arvold and Karen Schuelke,

my brothers Scott and Tim Olson,

and the 28.8 million Americans who live alone.

I especially want to thank my friends Adolfo Quezada
for use of his superb quotes,

Emilie Cerar for her outstanding editing,

and Sr. Mary Southard for the exquisite cover image.

Contents

Preface

HAVING never lived alone before, I remember how anxious and wired I felt those first weeks when I moved into my own apartment. Everything was new, significant and unfamiliar. The first time I took my own key and got my mail in the lobby, went to the nearby grocery store alone—and especially the first time I dropped my rent payment into the slotted depository box in the laundry room—caused ordinary life occurrences to seem unusually meaningful and poignant. Each new step felt like a major accomplishment that I rejoiced over as I began the unexpected transition to learning to live alone.

I listened to all the new sounds: the rustling leaves of a shade tree, the distant slam of apartment doors, the muffled traffic sounds from the highway and the whoosh of semi-trucks releasing air brakes from the gas station across the street. I began to learn that while I lived alone, the sacred, ordinary eternal rhythms that surround each of us surround us still—even when we move to new, unfamiliar places. We just need to welcome and recognize them as they reveal themselves in our new surroundings.

It is common sometimes for people who are learning to live alone to wonder, "How will I do? Who will care about me?" It is important to ask the questions, sink into the experience and feel the complex emotions. More importantly, it is vital to be receptive to the stirrings within us which faith and optimism offer. Whether you are leaving home for the first time to live alone in a college setting, beginning a job in a new location, are separated, divorced, widowed or unmarried—for whatever the reason—millions of people live alone and thrive. As in all stations in life, the unique dynamics of living alone bring its own challenges, lessons, joys and rewards.

As I learned to live alone, I prayerfully sensed that deep secrets—more life affirming than I could ever have imagined—waited for me. Perhaps the words of Adolfo Quezada sum up best what I grew to comprehend, "You face choices every moment of your life and every choice is an opportunity to take care of yourself. To love yourself means to make choices which enhance your spiritual good. Self love results in a sense of ownership for your life and a responsibility for your fate. Treat yourself as you would treat someone you cherish."

As we mature in learning to live alone, we find that there are hidden dimensions to this way of life that we didn't know were there. A dream I had reinforced this. I was walking through my apartment hallway and as I stepped outside, I suddenly came upon an intriguing path that wasn't there in reality. The path was carpeted with soft pine needles and led into a deep forest. I could not see where the path led but in the dream, I knew instinctively that it was to something wonderful, reminding me of Isaiah 42:16, ". . . by paths they have not known, I will guide them."

Though we may live alone, the confidence is ours that we are each guided and upheld by God, the voice of life and all we hold dear. Like many of life's experiences, living alone is a process that has little to do with an external or internal clock. These meditations may coincide with what you are experiencing at the time you read them. Conversely, they may not mirror your mood or situation in the way they are arranged; also, the four weeks of meditations, like our inner seasons of the soul, do not always follow a calendar month. So, let the spirit guide you to use them in a constructive way that is uniquely right for you. It is my hope that this book will offer comfort, inspiration and empowerment to those living alone. May your path be blessed with joy—wherever it may lead.

Week One

Starting Off

It is late, well past midnight;
your soul is at peace
as you reflect upon the significance of your life.

Tick tock—tick tock.
A nearby clock seems to carry a message.
Within its steady rhythm God speaks:
You matter—your life counts.
You are guided—your prayers are heard.

You think about the life journey
that has brought you to your present state of living alone.
You recall all the new starts you have made
and will continue to make through unfamiliar experiences.

Even though the future seems unclear
and God's timing as yet appears unreadable,
you find quiet strength and confidence as God promises:
All will be well—you'll find your way.
Secrets will be revealed—familiar faith will be your companion.

Day 1

✥ Remembering Those ✥ Who Care

"I do not cease to give thanks for you as I remember you in my prayers."   —*Ephesians 1:16*

As a summer breeze flapped the white shade on my apartment's screened window, it reminded me of a boat sail billowing on a lazy day. Letting my thoughts wander, inner peace drifted serenely across the waters of turbulent memories as I adjusted to the shocking collapse of my marriage. Thus began my journey as a single woman living alone.

Initially, a myriad of emotions tore through me, but within days I knew I needed support. I contacted a number of friends and colleagues and within hours, prayers and encouragement began filtering in. Immediately, I felt a shift inside that uplifted me beyond tears to resolve and clarity. It was as if a spiritual momentum gathered me close and unveiled what I needed to do each step of the way as I began my new life.

At the outset, I lived with my son and daughter-in-law for a month while waiting for my apartment to become available. They, along with my sisters and a close friend assisted me in practical ways when I was frozen with inertia and uncertainty. Rather than the world crashing in upon me, the world seemed to open up and embrace me as I contacted community services and found the financial benefits and support I would need as a disabled person making my way in the world and *living alone* for the first time in over thirty years. How those unfamiliar words haunted me at first until my sister helped me choose an affectionate Siamese cat named Tubby from the humane society . . . and "I" became a "we." I was no longer alone.

As I pondered the upheaval and transitions of that first month, thunder rumbled, jarring me out of my musings. Outside the sky had darkened causing the white globe street lights of a neighboring apartment complex to come on prematurely. A cool, refreshing gust of wind rushed through the screen and I raised the shade so that I could see the whole panorama of the advancing storm approach. Tubby perched on a table nearby, his paws on the window frame, as we both peered out in anticipation. As it began to rain, misting our faces, I was filled with gladness and a feeling of empowerment for the first time since my move. As a leaf tumbled by carried on the wind, I remembered and blessed all those who had helped me make such a pivotal change in my life and who I knew I could trust to be there through every storm I encountered.

Who are the people in your life who you would like to bless and extend gratitude to for being your shelter in the storms?

Love is the force within you that gives to others what you hope will be given you.
—AQ, Loving Yourself for God's Sake

Day 2

✤ A Promise of Things to Come ✤

In this you rejoice, even if now for a little while you have had to suffer various trials, so that the genuineness of your faith—being more precious than gold that, though perishable, is tested by fire—may be found to result in praise and glory . . .
—1 Peter 1:6,7a

That early summer, Kandiyohi, the county I moved to was experiencing the worst drought in fifteen years. The levels of the lakes were down and carpets of dried leaves laid in circles around the bases of trees, fallen onto the brown, bristly grass. Because of the severe heat, many area schools closed to conserve energy. Lawn watering and campfires at the state parks were banned.

Reveling in the sudden, drenching downpour as a promise of things to come, I listened to the loud singing of the bright-yellow finches attending a feeder outside my apartment window. At the time I had been in my apartment only nine days. Feeling nervous, uprooted and still too soon to feel at home, I had a sense of better days to come.

Feeling the need to stay in the moment and to be present to each day's unfolding, I decided to write out a mission statement to express my hopes:

- stay strong and grounded in faith
- conquer fear through trust in God's care
- surrender old dreams that I have outgrown
- give voice to my sadness and let it speak to me
- understand that acceptance of reality is the first stepping stone to healing
- seek personal wholeness and create a new vision of who I want to be
- remind myself often that it is my choice to take the high road
- decide that betrayal is not going to make me bitter or defeated

Like the dropped levels of the lake, faith temporarily felt as if it had receded from my inner shorelines as well. I could relate on a psychological level to the scorched landscape, blistering weather and need to conserve energy. However, the affirmation of my mission statement, the drizzle of rain and most of all, the riotous singing of the finches seemed to prophesize that the day was coming when I would end up singing louder than ever—stronger, deeper and more passionate about life than ever before.

If you were to write out a personal mission statement expressing your hopes, what would it be?

Let your decisions reflect the totality of your love for God, your faith in God's love for you, and the humility of your love of self.
                    —AQ, *Loving Yourself for God's Sake*

Day 3

✤ The Legacy of ✤
a Bridge Builder

I told them that the hand of my God had been gracious upon me, . . . Then they said, "Let us start building!" So they committed themselves to the common good. —Nehemiah 2:18

In the compelling poem, *The Bridge Builder,* Will Allen Dromgooles writes of an old man traveling alone at twilight who comes to a vast chasm. Weary and spent, he makes it safely to the other side. However, he does not travel on, but turns back and builds a bridge so that the pilgrims who come after him will have a place of safe crossing.

A number of years ago, I had a dream about a mystical woman who stretched herself across a treacherously deep chasm between two cliffs, creating a safe passage for those detoured by lack of inclusion and tolerance. Like the old man, she built a bridge for others—by becoming it herself. At the time, I did not realize the legacy the old man and the Bridge Woman would offer me as I stenciled the words: *To everything there is a season* across my dining room wall. Within a short time, however, I found myself walking a journey I'd have sworn would never be mine— and faith became the bridge that linked my old life to my new one as I began learning to live alone.

"Love is not like a faucet," I'd told my young adult children. "You can't just turn it off, even if you want to." At first I did not want to acknowledge this love; I was shell-shocked and felt that admitting it would be an act of weakness. However, as I moved forward, that love became a bridge and telling my children the truth about it brought a sense of unexpected freedom.

I never hid my distress from my children as I moved out of the family home into an apartment, but I was careful to monitor what I said and how much. I wanted to be sensitive to their moods and needs; this was the most important advice I received from mentors, who told me not to underestimate the depth of their reactions and feelings, no matter what age they are. I took this advice to heart and while I was not perfect in knowing what to say and when to say it, it proved to be a reliable bridge for all of us as my children and I grew closer than ever. More and more, I realized that whether we live alone or not, we are called to be bridges for our loved ones—linking our past and our changes in family dynamics with our future.

What are some ways that you are called to be a bridge of support in your relationships with others?

In your language use words that build, not those that tear down.
                    —AQ, *Loving Yourself for God's Sake*

Day 4

✣ Re-framing Beauty ✣

Jesus said to them,
"My food is to do the will of him who sent me
and to complete his work.   —John 4:34

Food for the soul—how I needed it during the first few months as I adjusted to my new life as a single woman. In *When Your Long-Term Marraige Ends*, Elaine Newell writes, "Down the corridors of time, human beings have asked the same two basic questions, and we still ask them today: Where do I find food? Where do I find love?"

As I learned that beauty is food for the soul, I recalled Newell's words often as I began writing down significant happenings that reminded me of the beauty in my world. Some of these included the Fourth of July fireworks I observed over the lake, a decadent chocolate dessert at a fine restaurant, a fawn that raced past my window, the sight of my brother-in-law and nephews wind surfing, sitting with friends at the beach while digging our toes into warm, white sugar sand, an unexpected smile from the boy who bagged my groceries, an enticing Pina Colada in a crystal goblet, the phenomenal sight of the moon turning a blood red during an eclipse, and many more memories.

Learning to live alone is initially a major life change. It takes some time to relax enough to mindfully take in beauty; however, the day comes much to our amazement and gratitude. Recognizing the miracle of burgeoning self-confidence is empowering as we come to realize that our personal happiness does not necessarily come through others but through our own inner wells of receptivity and resilience.

Those of us who live alone can view our lives as clean slates ready for whatever adventures await us. By choosing to honor life lessons and not allowing the past to define us, the promise of new possibilities and meaningful, sacred living is endless.

Where do you find food for your soul?

Do not expect a relationship with someone else to meet your basic needs. Your basic needs will be met only when you establish and maintain a relationship with God and with yourself.
      —AQ, *Loving Yourself for God's Sake*

✤ A Brave Question ✤

For I am convinced that neither death, nor life, nor angels, nor rulers, nor things present, nor things to come, nor powers, nor height, or depth nor anything else in all creation will be able to separate us from the love of God in Christ Jesus our Lord.
—Romans 8:38-39

Living alone allows a great sense of independence to do what one wishes when one pleases. However, the other side of the coin is that there can also be periods of loneliness when there is no one to bounce ideas off of, or share a victory or funny moment with. In adjusting to my new lifestyle, I had a tough time with a jumble of emotions all relating to loneliness.

Like waves lapping the nearby lake shore, these feelings washed and rolled over me as if I were a beach surrendering to the tides of my life. Each wave seemed to diminish me somehow—the rhythms of loneliness reminding me of grains of sand washing out to the deepest part of the lake, where it would settle until the next big storm stirred things up and changed the shoreline yet again. Several friends had written to ask me if I was OK, and I was tempted to reply, "No, I'm not," but soon after, I felt as if I were. It occurred to me as I reflected upon the paradox and temporary inertia I felt, that this was not a bad thing, but rather a natural ebb and flow following a major life transition.

Resting under a silky, black comforter with fur trim, I thought of all I had been processing since my journey began. The question that seemed to rise, fall and linger like a held breath finally revealed itself: "Who will love me now that I am living alone?" The summer breeze outside my window seemed to still and hush for a moment in the face of such a brave question, pausing as the tossing branches of the shade tree fell motionless. The sheer beauty and awe of life seemed to reach out to me as the words, "I will love myself" resonated from some deep, echoing well within. That afternoon, I understood more fully than I ever had in my life that I could send love to myself in a way that could companion me, uplift my mood and heal my wounds.

The love of my very soul for itself, God, my children, the nurturing small space I called home, my sisters, brothers, relatives and friends—even the presence of the shade tree and Tubby curled up at my feet helped mark another important rite of passage—as I moved forward one more day on my continuing quest into the Unknown.

In what ways do you reach out to yourself when you are lonely?

Sweet and gentle Soul, child of God, now is the time to let yourself be loved.
—*AQ, Loving Yourself for God's Sake*

Day 6

✤ The Source of Security ✤

They are not afraid . . .
Their hearts are firm, secure in the Lord.
—*Psalm 112:7*

When I first began to live alone, I remember being very concerned about my safety until I learned to relax. My friend Sheila Gales Biernat also experienced this fear, "I find I have a feeling of greater vulnerability. If something happens to me, I wonder if there will be anyone who will know it. Having a young son, I don't go jogging like I used to, because I wonder who will be there for him if something happens to me."

Sheila explained that one of the most challenging aspects of living alone for her was not having another adult to turn to and share various emotions she was experiencing such as joy, doubt, sadness or anger. She talked about missing physical and emotional connections like sharing the silhouette of a beautiful sunrise, cuddling on the couch, or laughing over something unexpected. On the positive side, Sheila, a person dedicated to a life of service, finds

27

that because she is alone, she can more easily suit her schedule to fit her mood, desires and pace.

The scripture verse, *"Do not be afraid, I am with you,"* holds meaning for my dear friend because "this scripture lets me know that although I may appear to be physically alone, I am spiritually tethered to a greater power that links me to the universe as a whole. I feel great comfort in the fact that God is near whatever or whenever my needs arise." Sheila advises those who live alone to enjoy the silence and special times you can carve out to be alone with God, "In the silence lies great potential for growth. Try to fathom how much God loves you and what His will is for you. Singleness gives you the opportunity to know God more intimately by devoting more time to meditation and discovery."

Talk about the importance of a practical security system you have in place as well as a spiritual one.

> *. . . we must pack for one and continue the journey by ourselves. When we let go of our reliance on the things of the world to protect us, when we release even our loved ones as saviors, we come to discover the one and only source of our security; we come to know God who will never leave us alone because we are a part of God.*   —AQ, *Heart Peace*

✤ *One of the Secrets* ✤

Rejoice in hope, be patient in suffering, persevere in prayer. Contribute to the needs of the saints; extend hospitality to strangers. —Romans 12:12-13

When I moved to my apartment, even though I was a complete stranger, neighboring tenants graciously welcomed me. One of the first persons I met became a special friend. About thirty years older than me, in her eighties, she and I share a common bond, which Ann of Green Gables (from the famous novel by Lucy Maude Montgomery) delightfully describes as Kindred Spirits.

When it comes to the art of living, my friend knows the ropes and through her example, I received several insights in how to live alone successfully. Daisy is very active and attends many of our community functions as well as doing volunteer work for her church and civic organizations.

Like many women who are senior citizens and who live alone, she is widowed and misses her husband deeply but carries on with the private dignity befitting a hospitable woman of inner strength who has been an inspiration to me. Daisy is devoted to her family and sees them often. She likes growing things, knitting, traveling and even camping.

A night owl like me, my friend and I slip notes under each other's doors in the middle of the night and sometimes she leaves freshly baked sugar cookies on my door knob. Once, when I was distressed about something, she slipped a pewter medallion under my door that had the word peace engraved on it, intuitively knowing I needed the message. Through my lovely Secret Pal and other men and women like her, it is evident that one of the secrets to living a full life as a person living alone is through reaching out to others.

Describe ways in which you feel you are called to extend hospitality to others, unique to your personality and life circumstances.

The love between yourself and God cannot be exclusively for you. It bursts from your heart into the world to do God's bidding.
—AQ, Loving Yourself for God's Sake

Week 2

Settling In

It has been a long week
filled with many spiraling thoughts.
There has been much to learn, process and make sense of.
You've felt overwhelmed one minute—
empowered the next,
Worn out one minute—capable in the next.

Your life is like a pendulum
swinging between many unsettling emotions.
You have begun the art of settling in.
You catch a glimpse of your reflection in a mirror.
Prayerfully attentive, you feel compelled
to take a closer look.

You feel drawn to your image.
As you gaze into your own arresting eyes
you realize that you are a sacred companion to yourself.
In the stillness of that deep knowledge,
God speaks silently to your enlightened heart:

> *Trust your instincts—lean on faith.*
> *Embrace the past—let God restore.*

✣ Spiritual Elegance ✣

See, the home of God is among mortals.
He will dwell with them;
—Revelation 21:3a

One of the beauties of living alone is that the space you live in is yours to define. Early on, I made the choice to view my living space as sacred—reflecting things I love, my personality, memories and values.

Because my apartment is small, I designed the rooms to flow into each other with the same sensibilities carried throughout. As you walk through a little hallway, there are three small wooden chests stacked on top of one another, with a crystal vigil light sitting on top from my Aunt Peggy. Hanging on a wall nearby there is a beautiful, fringed leopard shawl from my friend Melanie and a framed print of a mother and baby giraffe, given to me by my son Dana.

My goal was for my home to be a renewing place for myself, my friends and family—a comfortable place for body and spirit that inspired relaxation and a sense of well-being. Ease of conversation was encouraged by inviting guests to settle back on my three strategically placed hunter green leather sofas. A six-foot antique tapestry painting of a woman with her arms raised in prayer and nearby soft, white, fur throw pillows created a prayerful ambience that reflected the vision I intended for the space.

When I was setting my dining table with my new, stunning African-style dishes from my sister Julie, I felt flooded with a sense of joy and pleasure. I realized with a deep, abiding satisfaction that I love living with a sense of style and spiritual elegance that nurtures the soul. This has nothing to do with materialism and everything to do with living with intention in a place that inspires beauty, mindful living, creativity and passion.

How does the home you live in reflect your style, personality and faith?

> *Creativity does not venture into chaotic, busy places, but instead is born in a calm and restful nest.*   —AQ, *Sabbath Moments*

Day 2

✤ Lessons in Trust ✤

Well done . . . ! Because you have been trustworthy
in a very small thing, take charge of ten cities.
—Luke 19:17

To close down or retreat can be a tempting, impulsive reaction to fear of the unknown and the unfamiliar. Scripture is infused with beautiful passages that remind us to trust. These never spoke to me more deeply than when I began to live alone. Exhausted from the move and everything surrounding it initially caused me to consider discontinuing my ministry work, but much to my surprise, after replenishing my energy, I ended up expanding it!

When we open to the momentum of God's spirit within us as we process life's happenings, we find that our outreach voices grow stronger and more insightful; a sense of empowerment lessens the trepidation. We become cultivators of trust. As we set small goals and see them come to pass, we feel encouraged to set even larger and more daring ones.

Reviewing the goals I set six months before, I checked off the following:

- ✓ get my own place
- ✓ see doctor for a physical
- ✓ visit the dentist
- ✓ make a new friend
- ✓ learn to play cards
- ✓ pay my own bills
- ✓ have complete hair, makeup and fashion makeover
- ✓ lose weight
- ✓ find a church that I love

Marking each thing on the list with a red pen was very satisfying. When my sisters affirmed my progress by saying the old Joni was back and that I was 1,000 times better than I was before, I grew in trusting my own evolving capabilities and most especially in trusting God as a confidant, guide and encourager.

How are you progressing in learning to trust yourself and God?

When you allow yourself to be discovered in the light of God's love, this encourages you to develop your full potential. You adopt the necessary discipline to be true to your higher self and dedicate yourself to God, the source of all love.

—AQ, Loving Yourself for God's Sake

Day 3

✣ Finding Peace ✣ Through Imagery

The Lord bless you and keep you; The Lord make his face to shine upon you, and be gracious to you; the Lord lift up his countenance upon you, and give you peace . . .   —*Numbers 6:24-26*

My cousin, Roger has lived alone for nearly a decade and is an inspiration to me. Following the breakup of his marriage, he left a career he loved as director of a community theater and moved across the country to live near his two young sons. Not being able to live with them full time has been the most difficult aspect of living alone, he says.

When he spends time alone, Roger says he enjoys "winding down, introspection, meditation and making peace with myself and others." Fond of the beatitudes and the Parable of the Talents, the beautiful, poetic imagery of the Twenty Third Psalm is especially meaningful to Roger as is Monet's famous painting, *Waterlilies*. During times of frustration, he says images of ballet dancers, nature and wildlife art console him, reminding him that "We are never alone" and "This too shall pass."

One of my own favorite images is portrayed in an archetypal image by Sr. Mary Southard, entitled *The Journey,* that speaks of moving from the past to the future. Painted in a swirl of jewel-like shades of blue, violet and purple, the image depicts a mystical woman being carried on a white horse. Done in an impressionistic, free flowing style, there is a dream-like quality to the work that I find deeply spiritual and compelling. To remember and reflect on this image brings a sense of peace when I don't know where I am going in life.

Aptly titled, *The Journey* reminds me that we are all being carried through life by God and angels that bless us with their guidance and direction.

What touchstone images do you have that remind you to be at peace and to trust God in your life?

*Time is a river that flows through the ages. We can-
not stop it, but merely change its course; we cannot
possess it, only use it well. The water that passes us
right now is the present moment, the river is eterni-
ty. The peace that surpasses all understanding is the
peace that comes when we stop trying to figure out
what is going to happen to us, when we stop looking anywhere but right in front of us.*

—AQ, *Heart Peace*

✤ The Sign of the Shadow ✤

Isaiah said, "This is the sign to you from the Lord, that the Lord will do the thing he has promised: The shadow has now advanced ten intervals; Hezekiah answered, "It is normal for the shadow to lengthen . . .   *—2 Kings 20:10*

That first Christmas I lived alone was challenging, poignant and memorable. One night as I was writing letters I saw a shadow scurry across the wall behind my Christmas tree. Aghast, I watched as the shadow dashed momentarily back into view, looking like a giant tarantula out of a horror movie. Cautiously, I climbed onto a chair and peered among the Christmas tree branches. Nothing. Shaking my head, I forgot about the incident— only to see the same thing a few nights later. This alarming scenario happened a dozen times more in the weeks to come.

Finally one night while watching television in my living room lit only by the white twinkle lights on my tree, the now familiar shadow with many legs scuttled across the wall yet again. I knew I could not sleep another night in my apartment until I got to the bottom of the seemingly ominous visitations.

Crawling up onto the sofa arm, I stood on tiptoe, nervously scrutinizing the highest tree branches. And there it was: an exquisite spider about the size of a half piece of rice. It had spun a delicate web—barely more than a filament over the highest twinkle light at the top of the tree. Although I practically needed a magnifying glass to see it, the prismatic effect of the twinkle light caused the spider's shadow to appear fifty times larger than it really was.

Sometimes when we live alone, we imagine there are things out to get us that loom like huge shadows in our lives. Like the tiny spider's shadow, we inflate these troubles to monstrous proportions. However, when we spiritually surround our deepest concerns with prayer and trust—like the spider's web around the twinkle light—the reality of Christ being born into our hearts becomes the magnifying glass that lengthens the shadow of love in our lives. Through this joyous prism, the perspective of true faith enlivens our hope and calls us to flourish and grow.

What is a worry, doubt or self-expectation that you are blowing out of proportion?

> *Examine the demands you make on yourself. Are they realistic? Does the pressure to meet these demands take away the centeredness you need to live in peace?* —AQ, *Loving Yourself for God's Sake*

Day 5

✢ Looking Back ✢

And remember, I am with you always, to the end of the age. —Matthew 28:20b

On New Year's Eve I decided to review what I had learned as a person living alone. Looking back through my journal, I reread many quotes that had guided and sustained me. I've always found it helpful to mindfully and prayerfully pay attention to mistakes made, attitudes that did not serve, small successes and strength found.

One of the most significant lessons I learned is to take breaks from ministry work, practicing what is called a ministry of absence. Living alone, I practiced this often, withdrawing from my work and writing so I could rest, recover and explore my new life. I created a "new normal" as I studied books on embracing wisdom and coping with the disenchantment I felt when people I had previously trusted turned out to be "not who I thought they were." I also learned that forgiveness of self and others is essential, not because it condones hurtful behavior, but because without it we will never find the freedom in life to move forward in the world unburdened and unchained.

It was with great relief that I envisioned sweeping out the ashes of the previous year, the end of an age. As I did so, I proposed a toast to all things pure, white and new in my Book of Life.

Most importantly, I realized that endings, goals and new beginnings are the deaths and resurrections of our lives. If ever there was a prophetic word for me that New Year's Eve, it was, "Let the past lie in the past."

What is an ending from your past that you need to let go of and stop dwelling on?

Unforgiving memories haunt you and keep you trapped in yesterday. Forgiveness is the art of letting go. It is an ability inherent in the human soul to heal itself. —AQ, *Heart Peace*

Day 6

✤ The Ides of March ✤

But you, O Lord, do not be far away!
Save me from the mouth of the lion!
                                    —Psalm 22:19,21

March. It comes in like a lion and goes out like a lamb, so the saying goes. It is a messy, paradoxical month to be sure. Outside my apartment, there were ten-foot high piles of dirty, melting snow and rivulets of water trickling down the street everywhere and gushing off the eaves of the nearby grocery store. Some days it was extremely foggy and you couldn't discern where sky or frozen lake began and ended.

I was still in the learning stages of adjusting to living alone and a few days before, boredom overtook me. Impatience had her day, too, and on this day, like a prowling lion, fear and frustration visited me. Problems— specifically worrying about finances—knowing there was no one to manage my affairs but me temporarily shook my confidence. I forgot to count my blessings, forgot how

45

well I had been doing and most of all, as a friend reminded me—*I forgot to remember the Main Man.* As soon as she
said it, I realized that I was carrying all my concerns alone
and had allowed the messiness of life to shroud my confidence, just like the fog.

Like the lakes that would be opening soon, I knew that
the particular concern I was carrying could be left in the
winter of my life as I opened to new beginnings, learning
new skills and gaining self confidence. I vowed that I was
done feeling trapped by problems—and I prayed about it
with the deep, earnest conviction appropriate for someone who compassionately allows themselves second
chances and recovery. We must allow our life transitions
to imitate March—not only the month of many moods
and turbulent changes but the month of softening and
new life.

When you experience the messiness of life, how do you
open yourself to renewed belief in your capabilities and
God's help?

The more control you try to grasp, the less you have; the more control you surrender to God, the more under control your life becomes. Surrendering control doesn't mean you become passive or fatalistic. It does mean you trust that God has given you the physical, emotional, and spiritual tools necessary to negotiate life. —AQ, *Heart Peace*

Day 7

✤ Tools for the Journey ✤

*. . . let them repair the house wherever
any need of repairs is discovered.*
—2 Kings 12:5b

As the weeks of living alone turned into months, I humorously began to call myself Ms. Fixit. I filled a tool box with a hammer, screw drivers, pliers, nails, screws, extension cord, flash light, two kinds of glue, a tape measure, adhesive tape, scissors and a sewing kit—all purchased at a nearby hardware store. Doing this for myself added to my growing sense of self-sufficiency and confidence in meeting my needs.

I made fabulous living room draperies out of a designer sheet cut in half and secured with hidden tape and paper clips. When I broke the base of my vigil lamp tripping over Tubby, I glued and repainted the fracture with nail polish. Water stains on my bathroom linoleum from a previous tenant were custom disguised by dabbing the spots with cotton balls dipped in matching paint. When I ordered a clothing rack and it came unassembled, I got out my screwdrivers and put it together myself.

I removed a dozen amber crystals from an old, beat up candleholder and using a hole punch and wire, attached them to the shade of my safari lamp with spectacular results. I tightened drawer hinges, handles and chair legs and when Tubby left a claw mark on a tabletop, I re-stained the scratch with a tea bag.

The extreme pleasure and pride I took in fixing and restoring things and working with my tools proved to be a beautiful analogy to the psychological and spiritual tools I was developing as a person learning to live alone—as God helped me repair and reinvent my life.

Talk about the tools you have for making repairs and the tools of faith you have developed that help you navigate daily life.

Our faith must be in the effectiveness of the tools that God has provided. Our faith must be in the power of the present moment. Our faith must be in ourselves, who are capable of living as children of God, even in crisis. —AQ, *Heart Peace*

Week Three

Opening Up

The weather has been stormy and the night long.
As you look out the window
you see that the clouds have parted.
Prisms of sunlight streak across the horizon
as the sun rises over the land and in your heart.

It is morning
and a new day filled with possibilities is opening up.
"How can my life have come to this?" you wonder.
Despair has not had the last word.
Rather, the word of God has upheld you.
Independence has stretched you.

"See," God says,
You are rising through the days of your life
as I intended and hoped you would.

You have met the challenge—you have stayed the course.
Recovery is a reality—Wisdom is opening the way.

Day 1

✤ Getting in the Groove ✤

". . . for God all things are possible."
—Mark 10:27b

Feeling significant, finding meaning in life and feeling fully alive—these three elements can be considered barometers of a life well-lived. As I learned to live alone, I began to realize what joy can be found in fostering independence, stretching oneself and receiving new insights. For instance, I had no idea that there were so many people in the world who live alone. It never dawned on me—until I, too became a single occupant. Ironically, this very fact made me feel 'not alone' as I realized I was now by definition part of a growing, unique, universal community.

The truth is there are many advantages to living alone. I realized the great satisfaction to be found in enjoying your own company and being at home with yourself. I discovered a new sense of serenity in living in a very small sacred space that was manageable and beautifully organized. I had more time for pursuing my passions and ministry work, keeping odd hours and coming and going when I pleased. There was such versatility to my time and I found myself growing in creativity and empowerment for living.

When I found a church I liked, I remember sitting in the pew, gazing through the large walls of glass to a wild prairie beyond. It was snowing giant flakes that veiled the countryside, the silence beautiful and meaningful to me as I realized that I was learning the true meaning of contentment. To be at peace, in love with your life, family, friends and to feel guided by God—this I knew, is how life is supposed to feel.

Grounding myself by cleaning out Tubby's litter box, I chuckled—because I knew that daily chores keep life real—just like faith. Finally, I knew I was in the groove and getting the hang of what living alone is all about. I felt greatly pleased.

What greatly pleases you about living alone and brings meaning to your days?

You do not seek to discover a universal meaning in life but one that is unique to your individuality— your state in life, your personality traits, your circumstances, and the faith you have in possibilities.
  —AQ, *Loving Yourself for God's Sake*

Day 2

✤ One-Year Rite of Passage ✤

And when Jesus had been baptized, just as he came up from the water, suddenly the heavens were opened to him and he saw the Spirit of God descending like a dove and alighting on him.
—Matthew 3:16

When I went to visit my oldest son, Damian, I noticed his 1971 green GMC Sierra pickup parked behind his house. Once his decked-out dream machine, its rusting chrome bumper gives testament to the passages of his life—the inside cab, like a memory box, poignantly littered with my son's old, favorite things.

Now, as an anthropologist who works as a Transition Coach, my son drives a practical vehicle that serves him well on the road. There were times when my son did not think he would find his niche in life. Many challenges marked his journey, but like the thick layers of dust on the Sierra's dashboard, these integrated memories shape who he is today. When I look in his deep hazel eyes, there is a directness in the gaze, a clarity that reveals a passage my son has made: he has become a man.

Remembering the Father's words from heaven following Jesus' baptism in the Jordan river by John the Baptist, "This is my son of whom I am well pleased," one can well imagine the pride, devotion and depth of the words, which speak for every parent who celebrates a child coming of age.

When I commemorated the one-year mark of living alone, I realized I, too, had made a sacred passage. It now felt routine to get my own mail, go to the store, pay my own bills, create my own fun and walk familiar hallways. It was becoming more routine *not to worry* as compared to initially worrying about everything. This was the best part of my "coming of age" as a person living alone—not merely the absence of worry but the alighting presence of peace and a burgeoning sense of well-being, as I imagined God saying, *"This is my daughter in whom I am well pleased."*

What would be on your list of integrated past experiences that commemorate your own passages to successfully living alone?

> *At times when we are afraid or anxious of the unknown, we do not judge our feelings, but simply remind ourselves, "Whatever will be, I will handle it."* AQ, *Sabbath Moments*

Day 3

✥ *Come What May* ✥

. . . for now the winter is past,
the flowers appear on the earth;
the time of singing has come . . .
—Song of Solomon 3:11a,12

It was during the middle of winter—sub-zero temperatures and snowstorms one after another—that I came down with the worst case of influenza I've ever had in my life. Chills, fever, sore throat, non-stop coughing, severe muscle weakness and a killer headache. On television, the local news reported that this virus was so widespread and highly contagious that even nursing homes were closing their doors to visitors.

Too sick to read, watch movies, work on my computer, or even talk on the telephone, all I could do was lay in bed, miserably waiting for the sickness to pass. As a person living alone, there was no one to bring me chicken soup, a cup of tea or a word of encouragement. And because I certainly didn't want to expose anyone else, there was no one to drop by or ask to stop over.

Day after day, like the snowstorms raging outside my bedroom window, the virus surged through my body. By the time it ran its course, I had lost nearly ten pounds and it took months to regain my lost physical strength.

Enduring the course of that virus was a very tough thing for me. Looking back, I can see that there was nothing I could do at the time but float with the experience, surrender to the process and let nature take its course. Too ill to speak to God, prayer and faith became an unconscious attitude that carried me, even when the suffering, fear and loneliness oppressed me. Paradoxically, I felt a sense of peace, knowing I was in God's hands— come what may.

Talk about a time you had to prayerfully surrender to suffering or hardship, commending yourself to God.

In the midst of winter, the external falls away. There is nothing left to do but to go within and wait. My instinct is to search for the nourishment that will sustain me, and I seek it deep within.
—AQ, *Heart Peace*

Day 4

✢ Ye of Little Faith ✢

*. . . he restores my soul. Surely goodness and mercy
shall follow me all the days of my life . . .*
—Psalm 23:2b, 6a

I was standing at the sink in front of the mirror putting rollers in my hair when the oddest thing happened. Several of the rollers at the back of my head kept falling out. Using a hand mirror, I looked to see what the problem was and was aghast to observe that clumps of hair were missing leaving bald spots. In the following days, every time I combed or even ran my hands through my hair, an alarming amount of hair would continue to fall out.

A number of trips to my doctor, a dermatologist, biopsies and a battery of blood tests later, I was diagnosed as having Alopecia Areata, a mysterious auto-immune disease that causes baldness. In my case, it was most likely brought on by too much stress, a severe virus and rapid weight loss that disrupted the natural balance of my body's metabolism. In order to arrest the disease, the dermatologist had to give me multiple Cortisone injections in the affected areas.

I'd been through a lot of adversity and sorrow in my life and when my hair started falling out that winter, I was greatly upset and angry. "For God's sake," I raged at God, "Can't You even let me keep my hair? Haven't I been through enough?"

Despite my temporary lack of resilience and optimism, within a few months, my dermatologist announced as she examined the condition, "You are in complete remission and have experienced complete hair re-growth!" She said it was one of the most remarkable cases of recovery that she'd ever seen. As I celebrated, I kept saying, *"What a great day!"* As the word *remission* became my favorite new word, I wrote in my diary, "Winter's of the soul pass. What is done with time heals. God restores."

Talk about a time when you expected the worst and something wonderful happened instead. What did you learn from the experience?

We are not unlike the farmer's field that must lie fallow periodically in order to restore the lost elements and energy before it can be used again.
—**AQ,** *Sabbath Moments*

Day 5

✤ *A Party of One* ✤

*. . . they rested and made that a day of feasting and
gladness.* —Esther 9:17b

When I received the outstanding news that this book
you are now reading was of interest to my publisher, I was
ecstatic. I called family and friends who made plans to
celebrate with me on the weekend—however, it was
important to me to celebrate *immediately!*

Planning a dinner party for one, I went to the store and
bought the ingredients I needed to make a pot of home-
made chili. Back at my apartment, the aroma of onions,
garlic, green pepper, celery and tomatoes simmering was
divine. Accompanied by cheese, honey-barbecue corn
chips and a glass of wine splashed over ice, I savored the
moment and completed the celebratory meal with one
small luscious piece of cream-filled vanilla cake with
chocolate drizzled over the top. Then, I watched a favorite
movie, took a bubble bath and crawled into bed with an
intriguing mystery novel.

The thesaurus describes *enthusiasm* as feeling pleased, excited, exhilarated, eager, zestful, delighted and devoted. As I celebrated that night with myself, I felt affirmed and congratulated by God, as if He were saying, "See, when you are faithful to your talents and passion, you are leading the life I call you to."

As I meditated upon the joy I experienced in feeling like what I had to contribute was useful and a blessing to others, I realized that people in all stations of life—whether living alone or not—are called to live spirited lives, taking, as Adolfo writes, " pleasure in the gifts of life, in living abundantly," just as we ourselves "are the pleasure of God."

What are your favorite ways to celebrate good things with yourself?

Becoming enthusiastic again can happen when you reconnect with the love God has for you and the love you have for yourself. Enthusiasm means "with God" and God is love.
—AQ, *Loving Yourself for God's Sake*

Day 6

✢ Circles of Wisdom ✢

I, wisdom, live with prudence, when he drew a circle on the face of the deep, I was daily his delight, for whoever finds me finds life . . .
—Proverbs 8:12a, 27b,30b,35a

Making the best of living alone entails balancing living alone and being alone. Perhaps my wise middle son, Dana, who learned to live alone expressed it best when he described his recovery following an unexpected divorce, "I enjoy socializing as much as I enjoy spending time alone with myself; I appreciate both equally well!" Approaching living alone with an attitude of adventure, optimism and realism, he is discovering that just because one lives alone does not mean that you don't cultivate and expect to have significant, enjoyable relationships on many levels with others.

The first time I realized this was when I went to the county fair the summer after I began to live alone. It was a sultry summer night, clear and "close" due to the humidity—making the carnival lights, carousel music and noise seem surreal. I remember walking along skirting cables, eating delicious, greasy mini-doughnuts out of a bag, and picking a plastic duck out of a tank to win a prize. At the time, I wondered how life was going to go for me, as there were few certainties and many unknowns in my life.

A year later, as a second summer rolled around and another carnival, I could see that an incredible year of growth and discovery had changed me forever. I was a person who stood tall, presented herself with dignity, someone who extended and expected respect and who understood the privilege and joy of being alive. I had places to go, people to meet and God's calling in my heart. When I got home, I wrote in my diary:

Like a circle
I am complete, whole and significant within myself.
Whether I live alone or not
My days are in God's hands
And my worth and future beyond measure or compare.

Talk about the wisdom you have gained in living alone.

Our soul is the seat of wisdom, a wisdom acquired from life itself—from entering into the experiences that occur along the journey.

—AQ, Sabbath Moments

Day 7

✥ How to Take Leave ✥

. . . and I have been with you wherever you went. . .
—1 Chronicles 17:8a

The calendar on my table had X's on each day as I charted the count down to "Moving Day" when I would leave my beloved apartment that had been my home and sanctuary for over a year and a half. It was time to say goodbye and to offer thanks for the blessings and lessons I had received. A litany of thoughts and memories welled up within as I thought of all the passages I had made there as a person living alone and the victories that were won within those walls and in my heart.

Moving—going away—never to live here again seemed very strange. My apartment had been a spiritual galleon that bore me capably across oceans of uncharted experiences. What was unfamiliar, unknown and uncomfortable had become familiar, known and comfortable. I found fullness of life, serenity, confidence and happiness in this place.

Bags packed, the movers on the way, a memory came back to me of a puppy I'd seen months earlier, cavorting on the lawn outside my window. He had on a bright, red collar and had apparently slipped away from his owner. Literally bouncing with energy, his eager, enthusiastic puppy spirit could have put a grin on the most dour of observers. Laughing and getting caught up in the moment with him, I called through the window, "Here Puppy, here Puppy!" He jerked up his head with curiosity, ears flopping, and without hesitation, ran over to peer winsomely up at me through the window screen.

A wheat-colored Labrador, his pink tongue lolling out through what had to be a dog-grin, his clear, bright eyes peered into mine with complete trust and invitation. If he could have spoken, I know he would have called, "Can you come out and play?" Brimming with vitality, he was the most healthy, beautiful puppy I had ever seen. Suddenly, his ears perked up as his owner whistled and he was gone in a flash, romping off to his next adventure, fairly tripping over his gangly paws without a backward glance. It was as if life itself had gazed up at me through the window, eagerly inviting me to revel in the sheer joy of existence and the next new adventure just around the corner.

Broadly smiling, suitcase in hand, I closed the door and opened wide my heart.

If you were to plan an adventure for yourself, what would it be?

The soul loves to play. Through play we are recreated. We are not children, yet, we can approach life in a childlike manner, daring to be spontaneous. Be adventurous in your living and explore the unknown in the world. Stay close to God every moment! —AQ, *Sabbath Moments/ Loving Yourself for God's Sake*

Week Four

Moving On

But wait a minute.
You're thinking you might want to stop and rethink this
'moving on' idea.
You've grown so much, it feels good to stay in one place,
to enjoy one frame of mind.
The stability of familiar, routine, predictable days
has been a true blessing.

But now, yet again, God is asking you to move on.
"Why?" you ask incredulously.
More turmoil—more upheaval.
More uprooting, more re-rooting—who needs that?

By now, you've become accustomed
to having intimate conversations with God.
It comes as no surprise
when your familiar companion answers your questions:

. . . because there are more blessings waiting for you—
more important lessons.
More enlightening truths to unfold—more revelations of love.

It feels good to know that while you put your faith in God,
He puts his faith in you.
Whether you move on to new ways of thinking,
new relationships, or a new landscape,
that treasured bond of trust goes with you wherever you go
for all time—through all seasons.

✣ Opening the Door ✣

Look, I have set before you an open door . . .
—Revelation 3:8a

I moved to a house nestled in the deep woods with a distant view of a lake, following a reconciliation with my husband. Energetically, I went about the task of creating a sense of home in our new sacred space. However, my learning-to-live-alone days were not completely over. I was still alone five days a week while my husband commuted from his business on weekends.

Having embraced the past and all the valuable lessons I'd learned, I felt empowered, enthusiastic and complete—not because I no longer lived alone, but because I knew I could—and do so well. I felt a sense of ownership for my own life and my own happiness. I often thought of the famous painting of Christ knocking on a door that only opens from the inside. As I began my next life adventure in another new place, the spiritual practice of being an "open door" to life, God, loved ones and strangers was an aspiration I hoped to keep growing in.

Ironically, as I prayed to open my mind and heart on a deeper level, I kept a door in our house closed—*the door to the basement*. In fact, every night before I went to bed those first weeks, I uneasily propped a chair against the door. The unfamiliar creaks from the basement and the abrupt, loud knocking sounds from the boiler made me nervous and jumpy. My imagination would run wild at about 3:00 a.m. and fearfully, I would sleep with the lights on, expecting God-knows-what to happen.

Psychologically, because the basement of a house is underground and often dark, it represents the deepest realms of the psyche. You have to descend stairs to get there. Spiritually, I thought of the basement of my own soul where my deepest fears and victories are kept. After a few weeks, I felt ready to open the door to the basement and leave it open. Eventually, I grew completely confident in walking by the doorway at the top of the stairs or descending to the family room below—at any time, day or night—noisy boiler or not. This, I decided, is how we should feel about the deepest levels of our spirits, convictions and faith: it is best to not only leave the door open but to be at home there, coming and going freely and often.

If you were to imagine your soul as a house with many floors and levels, how would you describe the basement? Who or what comes to mind when you think of doors you have closed?

Open the door to your heart, enter in, and come to know yourself in all your reality.
      —AQ, *Loving Yourself for God's Sake*

Day 2

✤ *Invitation of a Rainy Day* ✤

Come, behold . . .
—*Psalm 46:8a*

It was raining dogs and cats. Flood warnings predicted up to five inches expected within a matter of hours. Even though it was only the middle of the afternoon, it was nearly as dark as night. As I walked briskly along in my rain slicker, the paved road was literally splattered with yellow leaves and in the near distance, the lake was gray and dappled from the downpour, the wind still and hushed.

I live on a circular drive and when I go for my walks, I call it *Walking the Circle*. Today without a soul in sight, water dripping off my hood, soaked from the knees down, I felt invigorated and alive. As I walked, I mused, "There is an energy that comes from walking the way; it invites you, wakes you up. You start noticing small details that lift you out of your lethargy or dullness of spirit that comes from being disconnected with the world around you."

The trees I passed looked silvery, slick and glistening on the shaded side where the mottled moss grows, while droplets of rain on the nearly bare branches paused like suspended transparent beads. I stopped at our mailbox and pulled out two soggy bills as thunder rumbled, waving cheerily at Jupiter, my little tiger cat watching from the window. It was a musical day and I could hear the intriguing sound of water plinking deeply into our well, reminding me of water dripping in a cave.

"What joy . . . " I thought, ". . . what joy can be found in solitude." Even though I was alone, I did not feel lonely. Quite the opposite, I felt animated. Loneliness can lead to isolation of the spirit, but aloneness with God and the vast world He created brings a sense of belonging and companionship. Even though you are just one, you feel included, enlivened and united with creation...at one with the source of all life, love and passion. From deep within the spirit invites: *Come, behold . . . join in!*

Talk about an outdoor experience you've had that lifted you out of loneliness to a state of well-being. When is the last time you went for a walk in the rain?

Fear of loneliness is fear of being separated, of not belonging, of not mattering, not feeling life. We welcome solitude because it is nourishing to the soul.
    —AQ, *Heart Peace*

Day 3

Drawn by Joy

Draw near to God, and he will draw near to you.
—James 4:8a

Just before Thanksgiving as I walked around the circular drive, I did something I'd never done before. On a whim, instead of walking it counter-clockwise as I usually did, I walked it clockwise. It felt very strange to be going in the opposite direction, even though I was walking the same familiar route along the lake, past the same houses and barking dog!

The route has several dips, shallow valleys and hills steep enough to cause me to be out of breath when I walk it. By going in the new direction—clock-wise—I found myself going downhill instead of uphill. It was a novelty to be in the flow of the downhill momentum, forcing me to run to keep up with the natural gravitational pull.

Grinning, I trotted downhill, caught up in the pleasure of the movement. Later I wrote what I felt God was saying to me as a Woman Who Has Weathered Many Storms:

When you felt as if you could not climb another hill or face another hardship or heartache, I was there cheering you on. I am always there, reaching out to you, reminding you: Peace in the Moment. Dream your dreams, expect triumph and joy, be touched by unseen helpers and guides who bring insight and wisdom. The design of your life and your destiny calls you to harmony, wholeness—serenity. Empower your days with faith, let it encircle and inspire your vision for living and giving. Your soul has a rhythm that tells you when you need to go in another direction or change how you think about something that is troubling you or wearing you out. Keep pace with my spirit within you. I have need of you—be ready, hopeful and available, tell people that for every uphill battle, there is a downhill journey that leads to strength, love and meaningful living.

As I concluded writing what I felt was God's message, I recalled a childhood memory of myself running effortlessly down the big hill in our horse pasture, hair flying, drawn along by an inexpressible force of joy and laughing in freedom and utter delight. The spirit of that young girl lives on.

When is the last time you gave yourself permission to change directions or allowed yourself to spiritually travel downhill for awhile?

> *. . . we surrender and let go of our resistance to what is. No longer do we try to control. We lay aside our armor; our mind, our heart, our soul, and our strength are captured by love's force.*
>
> —AQ, *Sabbath Moments*

Day 4

✥ Living Gracefully ✥

With great power the apostles gave their testimony to the resurrection of the Lord Jesus, and great grace was upon them all. —Acts 4:33

My magnificent, purple-plumed Betta fish, Gideon, survived his first near-tragedy two days after I brought him home from the pet store. The huge, brass mirror above the fireplace fell off the wall with a crash, knocking Gideon's bowl off the mantle and propelling him onto the kitchen linoleum with a whoosh of water. After I'd recovered from the shock and sprang into action, I dropped him three times because he was so wiggley. Within minutes he was back in the water, none the worse for wear, his gorgeous-hued, delicate fins rippling and fluttering as he circled gracefully in his bowl.

I keep Gideon in a vase-shaped bowl that has the roots of a live plant dipping into the water. Gideon glides among the roots, living off the nutrients, thriving alone in his home. An ornamental fish, Betta's belong to a group known as Labyrinth fish, because besides breathing under water, they can also breathe atmospheric air, like dolphins do. This adaptation came about through evolution as an extra respiratory system developed because of an oxygen-deficient natural habitat.

Observing Gideon, I can't help correlating life lessons for persons who live alone:

- Trust that when you get knocked out of your element, someone (our loving God) will pick you up and rescue you.

- Let the roots of your life grow deep; draw sustenance from your experiences and move freely among your memories, good and bad.

- Develop more than one coping skill for adjusting to life's challenges. Adapt to your circumstances.

- Let your faith evolve; let it be as the oxygen that gives you life; let the Holy Spirit breathe wisdom, insight and empowerment into your world.

Last but not least, as I observe Gideon lithely gliding in his fish bowl, I am reminded of the timeless beauty of a prayerful, graceful life that reflects the harmony of nature with its Creator.

How would you define a prayerful life? What can you do or not do to achieve this?

". . . All will be well" or "I breathe in love, I breathe out love," or any combination of words promotes heart peace. There is something soothing and comforting about repetition. Eventually, the prayer on our lips and tongue becomes a prayer of the heart.
— AQ, *Heart Peace*

Day 5

✤ *At the Mall* ✤

. . . and they shall be my people and I will be their God . . .
—Jeremiah 24:7b

There is nothing like a well-deserved rest after hard work and completing a challenging project. I'd been working day and night painting, wall-papering, designing and writing in between—when suddenly one morning I woke up realizing I'd met my present goals. Stretching languidly in bed, half awake, I fell back to sleep murmuring contentedly within myself as I drifted off:

There is nothing in my life that I can't handle.
I am completely at peace.
There are no worries worth worrying about right now
The present is good.
I am saturated with spiritual and physical well-being.
I am happy in this moment.

Later that evening while shopping for Christmas presents at the mall, the contentment lingered as I took in the sights and sounds of the holiday season. Humanity in all its diversity was present, along with baubles that glittered in every shop window. As I walked, my heightened senses took note of details that often get lost with the sensory overload of a crowded mall: a severely disabled man hobbling along pushing a cart, a young Hispanic man resting with eyes closed in a coin-operated massage chair, an old man reading a newspaper, children twirling around the food court sign pole, Santa and two helpers going over some paper work, vendors selling every type of gift down the center corridor, a Native American musician playing a haunting flute melody that faded as senior citizen "walkers" strode purposely by in tennis shoes.

Rather than seeming like a place of discord, I experienced a sense of harmony that I did not expect. Every person there had a precious, solitary life to live, and while sometimes you can detect the dissonance that accompanies the hustle-bustle season, those who feel joy spread cheer. At the check-out counter, a clerk looked me in the eye and asked pleasantly, "How are you?" Smiling back with a mutual spirit of good will, I replied happily, "Good, really good!" As she handed me my purchase and said Merry Christmas, I could tell she meant it—and so did I. As I walked out of the crowded mall and into the winter night's clear frigid air, my morning's beautiful affirmations came gently back to mind: *There is nothing in my life that I can't handle . . . the present is good . . . I am saturated with well being.*

Describe the inner dialogue you keep with yourself. If you were to create five brief affirmation statements for yourself, what would they be?

> *Move from the external to the internal. The real power lies there. You alone are responsible for your thoughts, emotions and actions. Treat yourself to the presence of others in your life. Be open to the gifts they bring, especially the gift of themselves.*
> —AQ, *Loving Yourself for God's Sake*

Day 6

✤ Twelve Luminaries ✤ of the Heart

Again Jesus spoke to them, saying,
"I am the light of the world."

—*John 8:12a*

On my fireplace mantle I have an artificial bouquet of stunning white tulips from my friend Frances, each with a white, electric light in its center. For the holidays, I wrapped the vase in gold lame paper and tied it with metallic gold ribbon. At night I sat alone with the lights low, reveling in the beautiful glow reflected in the mirror behind it. To me it represented the glimmering lights of illumination that came into being within me as I learned to live alone.

A dozen white tulips—a dozen luminaries of the heart. If I were to name each one, the litany would read like this:

1. *The Light of Endurance* that arrives as we learn that God sends us staying power when we need it the most.

2. *The Light of Shed Tears* that occurs when we express the truth in our hearts and allow God to comfort and transform us.

3. *The Light of Courage* that comes from being comfortable with fear and doing what needs to be done in spite of it.

4. *The Light of Optimism* that God instills in us when we expect the worst.

5. *The Light of Surrender* that comes from not rigidly resisting that which you cannot change.

6. *The Light of Trust* that continually reminds us that God heals all wounds and is with us when we suffer.

7. *The Light of Humor* that lovingly calls us to lighten up.

8. *The Light of Resilience* that encourages us to get back up when we fall and to keep on going.

9. *The Light of Patience* that says, "Take your time, think things through, don't make rash decisions."

10. *The Light of Maturity* that calls us to grow up emotionally and spiritually so that we can be all that we are meant to be.

11. *The Light of Vision* that inspires and intimately reveals God's purpose and passion in our lives.

12. *The Light of Love* that forgives wrongs, embraces vulnerability and whose strength empowers our every goal, dream, challenge and hope.

Talk about the lights of sorrow and joy you have known. If you were to name your own personal luminaries of the soul, what would they be? Write them down and share them with a loved one.

> *We count on inner knowing, rather than on concrete knowledge. In the darkness it is not our intellect that helps us but our faith. Our soul takes us to our most inward place, our essence, our core. It is here that we see the light.* —AQ, *Sabbath Moments*

Day 7

✤ *If All We Ever Say* ✤
is Thank You

How can we thank God enough . . .
—1 Thessalonians 3:9a

December 14, 2004, a diary page:

Thank you, dear God, for the wind today that blew across the land. As I watched the dark winter clouds race across the pale gray sky shuttled along by an Alberta Clipper, I was amazed at the velocity, energy and power. All that movement from one sphere thousands of miles away to another—if wind represents the breath of God— we were getting a mighty dose.

The sound roared through the trees, kicking up long-dead leaves on the ground in swirls, reshuffling the snow-dusted frozen landscape as if by the wave of a hand. Sometimes, God, I've felt that the reshuffling and rear-ranging in my life has been overdone and harsh. Now, as I look back and think about it, I can see that the mighty stirring that taught me to live alone changed and deepened my faith and convictions forever. Thank you, thank you, for Romans 8:28—for using all things for good in those who love You.

Thank you for blessing my life. Thank you for countless second chances. Thank you for encouraging me when I felt alone and helping me to frame my life circumstances and state of being through a transforming faith that became more real and honest than ever before. You taught me to find significance in the smallest of co-incidences, gestures of kindness and in the sacred spaces I called home.

Thank You for being a healing God of power and might, the listener and friend of my heart, a constant supporter through prayer and unconditional care. As I close the circle of this book, bless every person who lives alone and reads it. May each of us awaken to and recognize the reality of Your companionship through all the stages of our lives. Most of all, thank You for guiding us through the uprooting and re-rooting that shifts, rearranges and lovingly propels us forward through the spirit ever closer to fullness of faith and You. Amen.

If you were to offer a prayer of gratitude for the things you are thankful for, what would you say?

And so we pray, for prayer is remembering. We remember that we are the life of God in the world. We remember that love is our language...with great appreciation we receive the days you give to us.
— AQ, *Sabbath Moments*

Afterword

On April 10, 2005, as I reflected upon the vivid image of this book's cover, an amazing message was revealed to me, which I captured in my diary:

Benediction of the Night

There is a humming in the soul that comes—slipping quietly into the cracks of the human heart. There is a sacred music that rises through the depths of every wound. One night, while drifting off to sleep by my open window, night sounds from the Reflecting Pond crept into the room, ruffled across my skin along with the cool breeze and called me out of sleep. Drowsily, I listened to the symphony of the night that blended with the songs in my own heart, becoming wordlessly one.

"How could I have ever forgotten," I wondered, *"that all I am is lovingly merged with every ancient longing ever felt?"* I imagined all that I have experienced in life weaving like a tendril of smoke out through my window and into the woods, where it joined with the frogs croaking, the distant ducks quacking and the music of the stars above our beloved bungalow.

"There was never anything to fear," I thought. All the upheaval, soul searching, misery and pain become a part of the glory that is our eternal heritage. In the depths of our hearts, if we look deep enough and are willing to wait, the comprehension enfolds us—and one day, we know we have become wise—like so many who have gone before us. We can't help but count the scars and we think, "there have been too many." Yet within the same breath, we also know that there is strength and beauty beyond measure in the price we have paid. Drifting, I feel carried within the soul of God as the moonlight silhouettes the vibrant, secret world outside my window and in my quietly beating heart.

"It's all been worth it," I think in wonder. All the tears, hopes, yearnings to be my highest self, the patience, the sacrifice, openness and untold prayers. This night is like a benediction as in the stillness, the words of Psalm 42:8 linger, ". . . and at night his song is with me, a prayer to the God of my life." In that moment, I give myself over to the destiny of my life as one journey ends and another unfolds.

Additional Titles Published by Resurrection Press, a Catholic Book Publishing Imprint

For a free catalog call 1-800-892-6657

www.catholicbookpublishing.com